Dress Your Baby in Sage and Taupe

Dress Your Baby in Sage and Taupe

A HANDBOOK FOR THE SAD BEIGE PARENT

Hayley DeRoche

Countryman Press

An Imprint of W. W. Norton & Company
Independent Publishers Since 1923

DRESS YOUR BABY IN SAGE AND TAUPE is a humorous take on parenting, as well as parental consumer behavior and the marketing that feeds it. Names of products, companies, and institutions are either inventions of the author or are used satirically.

To Winnie & King, my sweet peas.
And to moms. This is a love letter to you.

Well, some of you anyway . . .

Contents

PART 2.

The Newborn Stage   53

(You are totally in control!!)

PART 3.

The Toddler Stage 85
(Someone else appears to be in charge now)

To Beige or Not to Beige

Welcome . . . to Werner Herzog's new line of children's toys: sad beige toys for sad beige children.

—*record scratch*—

Yep, that's me. You're probably wondering how I got here.

It all started—as so many things do—with a baby shower. You know how it goes—one minute you're shopping online, the next you're creating a viral comedy video about beige toys in the style of famous German nihilist filmmaker Werner Herzog that catapults your comedy career to new heights. Just normal baby shower stuff.

There I was, searching for a set of those classic rainbow stacking cups, and the algorithm, in all its wisdom, instead served me a set of neutral-toned stacking cups coupled with the most bleak, desaturated, sullen children "playing" with them in the marketing photos, and I simply sat, stared, and began to laugh. The cups were all beige, the children were all in perfect aesthetic beige outfits more befitting a funeral than a playroom, their eyes brimmed with ennui, and everything looked so gosh-darned sad. Behold: Sad beige toys . . . for sad beige children.

Okay, but why poke fun at an aesthetic? It's not that deep!!

Satirizing the beige aesthetic is about how playing with the way we live, laugh, and love is flattened by consumer culture; we see it in the popular "millennial greige" of modern houses intended to be as soulless as possible so they sell better, in celebrity clothing brands, and inside the homes of popular influencers; beige is the perfect neutral backdrop to help products POP on your screen, so naturally content creators flock to it like seagulls to a sandwich.

In a way, sad beige toys and sad beige clothes are the natural outcome from an aesthetic tied in many ways to consumption. After all, who hasn't felt the pull of the almighty algorithm trying to get us to buy-buy-buy in order to fit in and be on-trend? Who hasn't felt like if they just dress their baby like a Dickensian orphan that their child will be somehow more in tune with nature, that they'll frolic with spotted fawns and dance among the mushroom caps in the forest beneath a full silver moon, and (most importantly) that they'll get better AP exam scores someday.

So when you're standing in the home improvement store's paint aisle picking out nursery wall color swatches, you are contemplating very serious decisions! Will you choose khaki beige, executive khaki, or fingerling potato for the nursery? Everything is at stake here!!

As you put together the mushroom-cap-colored crib, you can rest easy knowing that you'll never give in to the syrupy siren call of plastic rainbow stacking cups and will instead curate exactly two minimalist educational wooden foxes carved by hand out of a hundred-year-old acacia tree. As you fold that tiny alpaca wool baby bathrobe in preparation, you should feel proud knowing you start each day with a warm bath followed by a calm reading of Mary Oliver's poetry, and finish with a moment of self-reflection during which your baby may—if they feel led by the spirit—compose a haiku (I have included several in this book for inspiration). Beige is the secret sauce to everything. All will be well with beige.

Is it really all so sad, then? All that sounds pretty nice, actually. Maybe I could go a little easier on the whole thing.

After all, maybe choosing the Sad Beige Life (SBL) is its own kind of love: A parent who cares enough to curate their baby's world has already ensured that their little one will be wealthy in a love that enriches and refines, a love that makes sleeplessly rocking in the nutmeg glider at two in the morning its own kind of gentle lullaby.

Picking out paint colors is a form of love, whether you choose beige, cinnamon, mushroom, desert, khaki, executive khaki (not to be confused with regular khaki), manuka honey, desert—but on a cloudy day, baked potato, fingerling potato, russet potato, or even something really crazy like sage. It's preparation, it's world-building, it's saying, *When you get here little one, I'm ready.*

So congrats to you, for choosing beige, for choosing love, and for choosing to buy sixteen copies of this silly little book to give to everyone you know. That is, of course, the biggest kind of love of all.

Now let's have some fun.

PART 1

Preparing for Baby

(dun dun dunnnnn)

25% loading . . .

How to Harness the Cold Embrace of the Abyss When Decorating Your Nursery

It is time.

The wind howls.

Rain falls in sheets of silver daggers.

Somewhere a screen door smacks against a solitary doorframe.

The signs and portents all point to the looming task drawing nigh:

Yes!! It is time to decorate your baby's nursery!!

This is the most magical time: when you undertake the project of preparing a room for your little one's introduction to this world—in neutral beige tones, of course. Beige is gentle and calming so your baby is sure to be cool as a cucumber. Here they will rock with you in the beige glider, cooing to your neutral lullabies. Here they will giggle (neutrally) and burp onto beige burp cloths. Here they will refuse to drift off to dreamland in their beige crib, choosing instead to scream like an inconsolable parade of firetrucks blaring their sirens long into the night. Aah, what bliss this room shall see.

To help get this room of joys and wonders ready, here are some must-have items to guide you, with their proper names.

☐ **STACKING CUPS:** Cups of Sadness—available in many exciting color forms!:

- ♥ Disassociation
- ♥ Inconsolable weeping
- ♥ Numb
- ♥ Bog
- ♥ Ennui
- ♥ Trapped in an endless spiral of madness
- ♥ A sky devoid of stars
- ♥ Puppy kisses!

☐ **CRIB:** Prison of Inconsolable Anguish

☐ **ROCKING WHALE:** Weary Watery Steed Rocking upon the Salty Waves of Infinite Tears

☐ **BALL PIT:** The Pit of Desolation

☐ **BEIGE TEETHING TOYS:** The world is a harsh place; there have been plagues, the consumption . . . bring all this to mind and more with the Tearful Teether, the perfect chew toy for your baby to learn of the pain of existence.

- ☐ **BEIGE SET OF IKEA BILLY-STYLE LOW BOOKSHELVES WITH PICTURE BOOKS NEATLY ARRANGED:** Deep Well of Wisdom. *Pro Tip: A library card is a must-have magic sword for your little one to carry them through the darkness, a true beacon in the dark night of the soul.*

- ☐ **TUMMY TIME DEVELOPMENT PLAYMAT:** The Flat Desert of Wallowing

- ☐ **CHANGING TABLE:** The Table of Ever-Changing Woes

- ☐ **MONTESSORI BELLS:** Ask not for whom the bells toll; they toll for *wheeeee*, musical fun!

- ☐ **FLOOR-LEVEL LONG MIRROR (MONTESSORI-STYLE):** Wall of Peering Upon Thy Cursed Visage

- ☐ **GLIDER ROCKING CHAIR:** The relentless push and pull of doom and destiny interlocked.

☐ **BEIGE MOBILE ABOVE THE CRIB WITH BEIGE MOON AND STARS:** Galaxy mobile to remind your child that they are but a speck of dust in the universe—a comforting thought in a way, as you make your way through life. It is a gift to know of one's smallness. Because what luck, what wondrous serendipity, to be so small and yet so very, very loved, when so many other lives were possible. Yes, existence may be fleeting, but look how full of love and joy it can be.

Best Shades of Beige to Ensure Your Little One Spends Their Days Pondering the Hubris of Man and Dreams Each Night of the Agony That Is Existence

EGG CREAM

UNCHURNED BUTTER

FROZEN LAKE OF UNSHED TEARS

HOTEL BATHTUB

MOLDY CHEESE

REGULAR CHEESE

CAREWORN PAGES OF MARCEL PROUST'S 1913 CLASSIC 'N WHICH 'E FAMOUSLY ROTE," THE 'NDS BETW'

TERMITES

In which Proust famously wrote, "The bonds between ourselves and another person exists only in our minds. Memory as it grows fainter loosens them, and notwithstanding the illusion by which we want to be duped and which, out of love, friendship, politeness, deference, duty, we dupe other people, we exist alone. Man is the creature who cannot escape from himself, who knows other people only in himself, and when he asserts the contrary, he is lying."

How to Win at Naming Your Baby

Traditionally, if you have a child, you're expected to name them something, instead of yelling, "AHOY, YOU THERE, WITH THE STICKY FACE!" across a crowded playground. Crazy, I know.

When choosing a name, it's important that you follow a strict set of flexible guidelines. The name must be unique, but traditional. It should be trendy, but not popular; classical, but also cool; vintage, but modern. Your child's name should be able to accommodate any career, from ska punk band singer to orthodontist. Boys should have tough names and girls should have ones that conjure up images of delicately embroidered Victorian gloves, unless you flip it and reverse it, in which case girls should have tough names and boys should have names that bring traditional fiber crafting to mind. These are the rules, and you must follow them if you are to win at naming your baby.

Oh, this isn't a competition you say?

Yes it is. Come on now.

Lucky for you, I have brought you a humble offering of baby names that will clinch the trophy for Best Named Baby. You're in good cool classical vintage modern unique trendy hands now. *You're welcome.*

Boys

BOULDERS. A WOLF HOWLING AT THE MOON. ONE OF THOSE OLD-TIMEY TOOTHY OPEN-JAW BEAR TRAPS. All of these would make excellent boy names. Boy names must be more rugged than a pickup truck commercial, grittier than a pot of grits bubbling over a campfire, and harder than a knuckle  sandwich. Okay *fine,* boy names can also be as gentle as a butterfly's cocoon, as sparkling as a river in June, or as fresh as a mint julep on the porch. Buuuuuuuut for the purposes of this list, these names are ones that will guarantee beard stubble and sideburns before your bouncing baby boy's first birthday.

For your consideration:

Scallop	Mackerel	Scurvy
Tarmac	Wallop	Brawl
Cannon	Whiskey	Brad
Granite	Bulldozer	
Barge	Bigrig	

Brainstorm Time! Add Your Ideas Here:

_____

_____

_____

Girls

J. R. R. Tolkien famously said that the words *cellar door* were the two most beautiful words in the English language. Girl names should follow this same logic. Don't let convention hold you back. The important thing is that the name sounds pretty, conjuring up images of sun-dappled buttercup meadows, or dainty lace doilies at Noonoo and Gazebo's house. A girl must be named something whimsical that reminds one of Anne of Green Gables, but not-so-plain Jane (Jane, on the other hand, is so plain that it's NOT plain; the girls who get it, get it). No, your girl's name must flounce and bounce like her Mary Janes as she jumps into another round of Double Dutch.

Wait, what was that?

A girl's name could be . . . anything? Even Bulldozer? Or Granite? Or Barge?

Heavens no. That can't be right. Here, pick one of these tender morsels instead:

Flotilla	Colloquial	Malaise
Allegheny	Marzipan	Ingénue
Morsel	Brioche	Susan
Lucid	Deliquesce	
Elixir	Tinsel	

Brainstorm Time! Add Your Ideas Here:

_____

_____

_____

Mystery Sad Beige Baby

If you aren't sure what flavor of sad beige baby you're having, but you know in your heart that you want to keep things firmly unique and on-brand, here are some obvious choices for your little bundle of beige:

Beige

Taupe

Fawn

Sorrel

Mushroom

Hazel (ALERT: Only one person is allowed to choose this one, so if you're reading this book, quick, claim it before someone else does!! All other would-be Hazels will be changed to Mushrooms)

Sienna

Biscotti

Parmesan

Tawny

Sandy

Shoelace

Tumbleweed

Percy

Bisque

Eggshelly

Brainstorm Time! Add Your Ideas Here:

_____

_____

_____

Grandma and Grandpa (Former Babies)

Babies aren't the only ones who need names! Grandparents have made it loud and clear that they are TIRED of being called boring old Grandma and Grandpa. Those names are fusty, musty, and dusty. Fair enough! Out with the old, in with the new old.

The rules of New Grandparent Names is that they have to sound either (a) wet and/or squelchy, or (b) like something sung at a polka festival, or (c) like names from a picture book, or (d) food. Bonus points if your choice ticks all the boxes!

Noonoo and Gazebo

Oompa and Boggy

Wormy and Puddleduck

Twinkle and Sprinkle

Mushy and Squishy

Ham and Cheese

Gnocchi and Orzo

Eldritch and Spoopy

Brainstorm Time! Add Your Ideas Here:

_____

_____

_____

The Entity

This is a great choice for those wishing for their baby to become a singular being untethered from space and time! Free your mind and let go into the void.

Transcendence   Om

Brainstorm Time! Add Your Ideas Here:

_____

_____

_____

An Ode to the Doula
I Found on Facebook

Seeking a doula in the greater tri-city area, budget-friendly (open to bartering!), chill but also passionate about being an advocate during one of the most intimate and transformative experiences of a parent's life.

You:

[replied with a picture of your foot]

How to Avoid Causing a Natural Disaster with Your Gender Reveal in Seven Simple Steps

STEP 1. Decide whose gender will be revealed. Will it be your gender? Your partner's? Your dog's? The sky's the limit! There is literally no rule that says a gender reveal has to ONLY be a baby's. So if you're planning a gender reveal for someone who's made more than one trip around the sun, these tips are for you, too. Everyone is invited.

STEP 2. What gender will be revealed? Are you planning a gender reveal for yourself? If so, great! You got this, Mama. If you're planning a gender reveal for someone else, the first step is to take a moment to appreciate what a good person you are. After all, parties are a real pain in the caboose to plan! Luckily, you are methodical and organized, have a great sense of style, and, also, your hair looks *really* nice today. You're gonna nail it.

Now comes the hard part: Accept that a gender reveal party isn't a party. It's a high-wire, death-defying stunt where you, the party thrower, are the ONLY PERSON able to prevent a full-on natural disaster. LOCK IN, BUDDY.

A gender reveal isn't just about making sure the bakery hides the right color in the cake or someone throws the right color Frisbee for Bailey the Goldendoodle to catch. A gender reveal is a cleverly disguised fire safety and ecological harm reduction seminar that, if done correctly, everyone will *think* is a party.

No pressure.

STEP 3. Select your gender reveal pedagogy. How will you relate this important news event to your guests? Despite very real concerns of wildfires, electrical outages, and/or floods, you can't skimp on pomp. It must be big. It must be bold. It must feature items from Crazy Todd's Explosion Shack. Sure, this has a strong chance of going terribly and irrevocably wrong . . . but also think of how good it'll look on social media!!

Some popular choices are:

+ Fireworks
+ Plane dropping smoke bombs
+ Olympic torch
+ Cannons shooting custom cannonball colors. *Pro Tip: Bowling balls come in many exciting colors, like Winter of Our Discontent Eggshell or Slow Spiral into Insanity Sage!!*

(PSA: The editors of this book would like to stress that for legal reasons this is a joke and you should not shoot any bowling balls out of any cannons.)

STEP 4. Send invitations to party-goers and local first responders. This is critical, especially if you've chosen to tempt fate with any extremely dangerous hazards, such as listed in step 3. After all, early mitigation is SO important when making reckless—I mean CUTE—viral gender reveal plans. Let the firefighters at your local

station know there will be cake and maybe a giant fireball that causes catastrophic, irreparable damage to the local flora and fauna. Here are some helpful wording suggestions you can adapt to your needs:

+ Your presence is your present! But we do recommend bringing a first aid kit and at least three gallons of water per person!
+ BYOLDFH: Bring Your Own Large-Diameter Fire Hose!
+ Pink or Blue, We'd Love You to Know the Best Way to Put Out a Rapidly Growing Wildfire Set Off by Explosives, So Please Attend a Safe Detonation and Extinguishing Class Before the Big Day!

STEP 5. Cake flavor selection. I once had a strawberry basil ice cream cake that was so good it haunts me to this day. So crisp and sweet, so summery and juicy, with just a little kick of zest from the basil, and the graham cracker crust was heavenly. You should pick that.

30

STEP 6. Outfits! If you're the one expecting, then you can never go wrong with a flowy, billowy Grecian-style dress (beige, obviously). Personally, I went with a dark and mysterious shroud as an homage to the unknowable black chasm of space and the infinite abyss to which we are all headed in the end. But coral is also nice.

For guests, I suggest sturdy flame-resistant pants and tops that meet NFPA standards. For those more comfortable in formal wear, you can't go wrong with a fireproof duster in butter or bumblebee yellow, and steel-toed boots.

STEP 7. Final emergency response prep! The day is here, the weather's clear, and the guests have arrived in their fire-resistant gear! Make sure they store their water jugs in an easily accessible location at the party venue. Designate a special picnic table just for this, with a red and orange tablecloth or balloons to help denote its critical function. The EMT and local fire departments have also arrived and have parked in the spots you've reserved for them as close to the explosive detonation area as possible; it's good to make sure that the picnic pagoda that you book is one close to a fire hydrant. And of course, gifts, cake, and libations should be neatly stacked as far away from the Fire Danger Zone as possible.

And now, a toast!! To you, and whoever's gender is being revealed, may this day and all the days after be blessed and disaster-free in . . . 3 . . . 2 . . . 1 . . .

Dear Abyss

 Parenting advice columns can help solve many problems, but just one can answer with the profound truths that only a great gaping Abyss can truly know. When you want real answers to real existential crises (including but not limited to weaning, teething, and birthday party invitation etiquette), write or call up *Dear Abyss*. Remember, no desperate plea to the infinitely unspooling ribbon of the universe is too small!

Dear Abyss—

Thank you for calling Dear Abyss, *your advice lifeline for all the parenting questions you were too afraid to ask a mere mortal.*

Due to a higher-than-normal volume of screams into the void, all of our Abyss representatives are currently pondering the futility of existence with other callers. Please hold until the next available Abyss is able to assist you.

This call may be monitored or recorded for quality Abyss purposes.

Please continue to hold...

Please continue to hold...

Please continue to hold. We promise that your looming existential parenting crisis is very important to us...

Baby Shower Advice

Sleep when the baby sleeps / sleep when the baby sleeps / sleep when the baby sleeps / sleep when the baby sleeps / sleep when the baby sleeps / sleep when the baby sleeps / sleep when the baby sleeps / sleep when the baby sleeps / cry when the baby cries / sleep when the baby sleeps / scream when the baby screams / sleep when the baby sleeps / throw up in your hair when the baby throws up in your hair / sleep when the baby sleeps / trauma dump when the baby trauma dumps / "dump" could mean two things here and both of them are meant to be implied / drive to work exhausted when the baby drives to work exhausted / pump in a non-OSHA-compliant janitor's closet with a security camera

trained on you when the baby pumps in a non-OSHA compliant
janitor's closet with a security camera trained on them / sleep
when the baby sleeps / clap when the baby claps / smile when the
baby smiles / drive to work and get fired when the baby drives
to work and gets fired / bring a lawsuit when the baby brings a
lawsuit / sleep when the baby sleeps / giggle when the baby giggles,
jiggle when the baby jiggles, win the lawsuit and vow to advocate
for working parents so your own baby can have it easier someday
when the baby wins the lawsuit and vows to advocate for working
parents so their own baby can have it easier someday / sleep when
the baby sleeps

Haiku Dedicated to the Lady at the Grocery Store Who Looked at My Body with Such Bright-Eyed Joy and Asked, "Twins?!"

No. No. No. No. No.
No. No. No. No. No. No. No.
Why would you say that??????

Dear Abyss

Thank you for holding . . .

Welcome to Dear Abyss, your advice life-line for all the parenting questions you were too afraid to ask a mere mortal. What is your question, my child?

Dear Abyss,

I'm having my first child and am overwhelmed by everything I'm supposed to decide, and the stakes feel so high! Montessori vs. Waldorf, baby sign language vs. telepathy, college vs. trade school . . . . It's all so much, yet if I choose wrong, it feels like I'll ruin everything. You're an all-powerful timeless entity existing outside the realm of space and time, and I thought you'd be just the right . . . thing . . . to ask for guidance. So! What's your number one piece of advice for new parents who want to give a child the very best start in life?

Sincerely,
Expecting the Best

Dear Bestie,

In life, there is no start, just as there is no end. Think of life less like a race and more like an undulating ribbon weaving a mysterious design out of the fibers of life.

A new child is thus an old child, and an old child, forever a new one. You, too, are thus both a new parent, as fresh-faced and dewy-eyed as your little one will be upon their arrival, and ancient as the hills.

Given all this, the best way to give your child a good start in life is to continue as you are going, but double it. For just as your love is doubling with this new family member, your example of goodness can be multiplied as an example for them.

If you gift a dollar to someone in need, next time give them two.

If you howl at the moon, howl twice as loud.

And if you look up at the stars and ponder the inexplicable smallness of yourself in relation to the everexpanding universe, ponder that smallness with double the awe, and double the gasps at the falling stars that pass before your eyes.

DRESS YOUR BABY IN SAGE AND TAUPE

See how the shooting stars have doubled in your eyes and your babe's wee eyes, as well.

Let the ribbon of time unfurl as it may.

Let the stars fall.

All will be well.

Cheers,
The Abyss

In Your Inbox:
Don't Miss This Sale!! Or Else!!

Flotilla + Barge <Flotilla+barge@marketing.com>
To: desperateparent@sadbeigeparent.com

flotilla + barge

Hi [<<YOUR NAME HERE>>]!!

It's me, your bestie over at Flotilla + Barge, your one-stop-shop for all things baby, and I'm here with a SUPER SNEAK PREVIEW of our BIGGEST SALE OF THE DAY. Since we're like sisters to each other, I thought I'd share it a widdle bit early, so you can get first pick!! [<<YOUR NAME HERE>>], you are my FAVORITE customer.

So hurry!! These deals expire in 27 seconds, so act fast, and use code INEEDIT at checkout for 10% off any order over $350.

The Cozy Shepherd Bathrobe: Made from the wool of the sheep your wee one counts every night to fall asleep, our Cozy Shepherd Bathrobe is guaranteed to keep your little lamb extra comfy in their sojourn from the bathtub all the way to the nursery where they'll get changed into bedtime jammies. Priced at only **$485**, you'll want to act fast! Now, you may be asking yourself if you could just bundle them up in their cuddly bath towel for the three steps from Point A to Point B. And the answer is sure, if you hate your baby. But for all the other mothers out there who actually LOVE their precious lambs, click now to add to cart.

Estimated number of uses: 2

The Heirloom Wipe Warmer: For generations, babies' behinds have enjoyed warm wipes delivered in our sleek, modern, and timeless diaper wipe warmer. Crafted from ethically harvested bird songs and fairy

fingernail clippings, your child's caboose will never know the cold misery of a normal wipe. Or, as we call those here at Flotilla + Barge, a peasant wipe. Your baby's bum will be the finest bottom in all the land, and you'll be able to rest easy knowing that when they grow up, you can send the Heirloom Wipe Warmer off to college with them. Buy now and we'll toss in the Heirloom Diaper for free! Cherish even the biggest blowout for a lifetime. **$742** (bare bones) || **$839** (deluxe).

The Snügasa Büginarug eStroller: Roll into library storytime in style with the Snügasa Büginarug eStroller, newly updated to include Bluetooth and speakerphone capabilities. For a very low cost that we're not going to mention yet in the ad, you can enjoy the effortless ease of eBike technology in your stroller. Simply charge your Snügasa in one of our patented charging ports located in many neighborhoods across the country, then choose your buggy speed, and go! (Speeds include Stroll, Meander, and Chased by the Hopes and Dreams That You Had as a Child and Never Achieved.) Other top-of-the-line features include a sign that says *I Need You to Know I Paid $9,200 for this eStroller;* real vegan leather seat; and fold-up technology that works the same way making a balloon animal works: Watch really closely about 18 times, and you still won't get it.

Note: Charging ports are currently located in Los Angeles, New York, and Appleton, Wisconsin; check back for more Snügasa-friendly locations soon!

- ♥ Stuff!
- ♥ More stuff!
- ♥ Stuff! Stuff!! Stuff stuff stuff stuff stuff!
- ♥ Stuff to register for your shower
- ♥ Stuff to make you feel empowered
- ♥ Stuff to make you feel prepared
- ♥ Stuff to make you feel less scared—

Yes, all this stuff is guaranteed to gently pave over the human experience lurking just below the surface. You know the one—the small knot of worry that asks, "Will I be enough?" and "What if I mess up?" and "Can I carry this weight?"

Well, act now, and when you add a Snügasa eStroller to your cart, we'll throw in a FREE ***JUST BREATHE MAMA*** print, suitable for framing.

Don't think about the weight of treading the path of parenthood that so many humans have walked before. Don't think about the fact that before there were bathrobes, or diaper wipes, or strollers, there were hands and hips and backs and friends and a village and, okay, also the plague, but you get what I'm going for here. You will figure out how to carry this weight. (Both the baby, and the existential kind.)

The weight will soften. You will find your rhythm rocking that babe in your arms, the gentle lift and swing arcing like the stars wheeling forever in the night sky, spanning space and time. The baby bathrobe will hang forgotten on its hook, the wipe warmer will hum in the dark, the stroller will sit by the door indistinguishable from the other neighborhood strollers cast in shadow beneath the porch lights. Everything will feel infinite. Everything will feel as though all the moments in time have led to this moment, of you, sitting in the rocking chair, cuddling your little one, as the world spins on.

[<<YOUR NAME HERE>>], you've got everything you need already.

You always have.

You always will.

Haiku Dedicated to Buying the Stuff from the Baby Registry That Nobody Bought for the Shower

I'm grateful no one
Bought the size small Boob Leak pads
'Cause now I need large

Sad Beige Deep Breathing

Helpful mantras for deep breathing during labor (or bureaucracy!):

Inhale: I am a powerful warrior
Exhale: THE UNIVERSE IS VAST AND FULL OF EXPERIENCES BEYOND MY COMPREHENSION

Inhale: I am a fearless fighter
Exhale: CHAOS AND AGONY MAY DEFINE THE EXISTENTIAL HUMAN EXPERIENCE, BUT I AM FLOATING ABOVE THAT NOW, LIKE A SMALL SHIP BOBBING ON A SEA OF TRANQUILITY

Inhale: My mind is a meadow and there are many flowers
Exhale: FEAR AND DREAD MAY GNAW AT MY BONES, SEEKING THE SWEET MARROW BURIED DEEP WITHIN, BUT I AM NO TENDER MORSEL AND I SHALL NOT BE DRAGGED TO ANY CAR-RION BIRD'S HIGH NEST, FOR I AM THE CARRION BIRD, I AM AN EAGLE, I AM THE FALCON HIGH IN THE SKY OVERLOOKING ALL I SURVEY

Inhale: My body knows what it is doing
Exhale: MY BODY BETTER KNOW WHAT IT'S DOING BECAUSE I'M BEGINNING TO HAVE MY DOUBTS

Inhale: The gentle babbling brook of my soul is guiding me
Exhale: TIME IS A TAPESTRY, WOVEN AND EVER-WHIRLING; THE STARS SPIN IN THE NIGHT SKY LIKE A KALEIDOSCOPE MORE ANCIENT THAN THE FIRST BREATH ON LAND; CAVES DEEP

BELOW THE MOUNTAINS LIE SILENT WITH UNSEEN GEMS AND JEWELS, DESTINED NEVER TO SEE THE SPARKLE OF EVEN ONE STAR, DESTINED TO FOREVER BE IN DARKNESS—BUT I WILL SEE LIGHT, I WILL BE LIGHT, I WILL SEE THIS THROUGH AND COME OUT THE OTHER SIDE BRIGHTER THAN ANY UNEARTHED GEM FROM ANY TIMELESS UNDISCOVERED CAVERN, BRIGHTER THAN ANY STAR; I AM TIMELESS, I AM PART OF THE TAPESTRY NOW, AND FOREVER, UNTIL TIME ITSELF IS MEANINGLESS

Inhale: &%&^*&%@!!$*&*^&*#@%^&&@^((!1
Exhale: . . . yeah that about sums it up

DRESS YOUR BABY IN SAGE AND TAUPE

Enough

This is it.

You made the birth plan.

You went to the birth classes.

Or maybe you didn't!

You found a hospital, or a midwife, or a birthing center, or something else that works best for you. Maybe you are going to a courthouse! There are so many equally wonderful ways to become a parent. The point is, you have arrived at your destination. Well, almost.

Clothes, check; cozy socks, check; your phone charger, check; a few books in case you get bored; your trusty harmonica; maybe some freeze-dried astronaut ice cream repackaged as "New Mama Fuel."

You've got the letter board for the Instagram post, you've got the booties and then a going home outfit and a nursing pillow and diaper warmer and an eight-foot-long hand-woven babywearing wrap with a design that was only made for two months as a limited edition print.

Obtaining this wrap was a quest that sent you tumbling down a million internet rabbit holes, trying to find one anywhere. You checked the usual big box stores, nothing; you searched boutiques, nada; you set internet alerts for if anyone posted one to resell. Nothing. The eight-foot-long hand-woven wrap was quickly becoming your white whale. Or maybe it wasn't a wrap, but a going home outfit, or lovie, or just the right crib. Just the right big kid bed. Just the right butt cream.

But the search never ends, even when you close the browser tab. You could click on a baby swing ONE time, and it will latch on to you like a tick and follow you around the internet for five, six, seven, eight, then nine months. Years. A millennia spent clicking away sidebar pop-up ads for—

FINISH CHECKING OUT YOUR *Snügasa Büginarug eStroller* NOW

HI [*your name here*]! YOU WOULDN'T ABANDON A CART IN A PARKING LOT WOULD YOU??? THEN WHY WOULD YOU ABANDON YOUR CART IN OUR BOUTIQUE??? CLICK NOW TO FINISH CHECKING OUT YOUR *Snügasa Büginarug eStroller* NOW. REMEMBER, BABY BRIOCHE WILL NEVER AMOUNT TO ANYTHING IF YOU DON'T BUY THE *Snügasa Büginarug eStroller.* USE CODE BUGGY10 FOR A TEPID 10% OFF THAT WON'T EVEN COVER THE SHIPPING AND HANDLING!!

Well that seemed oddly personal. And how did they know your baby's name? Was the Snügasa some kind of bewitched object, bound to you forever and a day? The thought wriggles around in your brain, a wily little noodle of concern. Did the soothing stroller follow you to the ends of the internet because you wanted it, because it was a glitch, a weird bit of information that clung to you like a barnacle, or did it follow you in pursuit, like a predator stalking its prey? Well, maybe not that serious. But also maybe exactly like that.

Because what is an expectant parent to a company, if not prey? If not, essentially, a mark?

They know all you want for your baby is to be safe and loved and destined for greatness. It's what every parent wants. What parent doesn't want the best for their child? It's a tale as old as time, and with good reason! But this desire—coupled with the pressure of Getting It Right—is like chum in the water to businesses. They smell the scent of your money through all the internet tubes, and they use it to funnel you toward their products, pulling you in with their sweet siren songs reminding you that you are nothing without the eStroller, or the wrap, or the going home outfit, or the organic wooden blocks carved from a thousand-year-old sapling. (Doesn't that sound good, even though it is technically impossible for a tree to be both 1,000 years old and a baby sapling?) Everything that could point your child in the direction of a fulfilling, successful life can be found, they insist, in this one set of silk scarves.

They know what you want is ephemeral and complex, and they know they can't really give that to you, but gosh darn it, they sure are going to try and pretend that they can. Everything you want is just a simple "add to cart" click away. Little baby [BRIOCHE] will be fine, because you bought this, and that, and that.

But here's the secret.

They are wrong.

Yes, there are things to buy that are necessary—a safe car seat, a safe way to sleep, clothing, whatever you need to keep them fed. But even these things can't promise a perfect life, or even just sleeping through the night. (Okay, anyone who's experienced the gulag of new baby nights knows there is nothing "just" about a good night's sleep. But I digress!)

Companies are going to try to get you to buy a lot of things, insisting that THIS will be what makes your parenting a breeze; STEP RIGHT UP and see the amazing Montessori acorns that will guide your child like Hansel and Gretel bread crumbs toward the path we desire for them. Buy this baby bathtub tool and clean your baby without ever touching them! For some reason!! Buy the New Mama Fuel That Is Definitely Not Just Repackaged Astronaut Ice Cream Like They Sell at the Museum Gift Shop, because when you're a new mama, you need the Right Fuel or else your child will not launch into life properly. Buy buy buy to secure their future!

Of course that's ridiculous; your child's future is not for sale. You can't add it to any cart.

Your child's future is in your arms. Their future is gliding back and forth through another long night in the nursery, it's in baby storytime at the library, it's on a picnic blanket at the park on a sunny day to watch the ducks. Your child's future is hoisted up high on your shoulders (sooner than you think) looking out at whatever you're facing together. You and your love are the most valuable things, and no company can ever sell something to replace it. You are what they need to thrive. Just you. When the ads scramble to ensnare you with their lies, when the stores send you six email reminders a day that you aren't really ready for parenthood without buying their remote-controlled combination

DRESS YOUR BABY IN SAGE AND TAUPE

night-light/AI lullaby generator ("learns your baby's name in under ten attempts!"), remember: You are who your baby needs. Not some AI lullaby generator, not a baby book that tracks every hiccup (don't miss a burpy minute!!). Just you.

And now is your time to shine. You've got your birth plan, your forms, your court date. And you've got yourself. And you, dear heart, are enough.

PART 2

The Newborn Stage

(You are totally in control!!)

50% loading . . .

Back Home

It's just you and me kid
Here in the nursery
The mobile above your crib turns slowly
Tiny cosmos distilled
Bitty stars dangling from strings
Twin moons parallel
We are so small
Yet somehow limitless
Luminous

Like when acclaimed German filmmaker Werner Herzog said: *Glowing . . . unimaginable stellar catastrophes take place, entire worlds collapse into a single point. Light can no longer escape, even the profoundest blackness would seem like light and the silence would seem like thunder. The universe is filled with Nothing, it is the Yawning Black Void. Systems of Milky Ways have condensed into Un-stars. Utter blissfulness is spreading, and out of utter blissfulness now springs the Absurdity.*

This is the situation.

So luminous—so absurdly, wildly, luminous.
Together.

Aesthetic Color Chart of Baby Barf

Ew, why would someone do that?
Stop it immediately.

Code Names to Use for Your Baby Online so They Inherit a Clean Never-Been-Used Internet Slate

You wouldn't give a baby just any old name, so why wouldn't you be creative with their fake internet one? Behold, a most bountiful harvest of perfect pseudonyms you can use to refer to your child online so they grow up with a clean slate. (Sure, they'll probably dash the clean slate to smithereens in a single day on Reddit, but hope springs eternal, and we really move in the direction of hope!)

+ **Baby Yaga:** Great for baby witches.

+ **My Large Cat:** Never explain, no matter how weird it gets. Of course My Large Cat Loves Mommy and Me Swim at the Y. This week My Large Cat Loves Breastmilk! My Large Cat Bit a Kid at the Playground; book recommendations for teaching NO BITING appreciated!!

+ **President Abraham Lincoln:** Great for search engine optimization, bad for whoever uses AI to write a paper, which honestly is another tick in the "pro" column for this one.

+ **COMING TO THEATERS THIS SUMMER: *BAA BAA BLACK SHEEP*. TAGLINE: *HAVE YOU ANY WOOL?*:** This one's a real game changer. Your baby's placeholder name is prime advertising real estate; sell your baby's online moniker to the highest bidder for fun and profit! Bonus: With simple find and replace technology, you can sell and resell the same space, just like a rotating billboard! That's passive income, baby!

✤ **The Reverend:** Imbue your child's online identity with an air of sagely monkish wisdom beyond their years.

✤ **Dumpling:** Cute, although don't be afraid to branch out and try other foods or inanimate objects. For example, you could also try **Sardine, Stinkbug, Emergency Exit Aisle,** or **Bunion.**

✤ **Leonardo da Vinci:** This won't inflate your budding artist's ego at all! Plus, if you have more kids, you can go full Ninja Turtles and keep the bit going.

✤ **President Benjamin Franklin:** Blog traffic low? No problem, you know what to do. It's time to toss some rage-bait chum in the waters so people rush to the comments explaining that Benjamin Franklin was never president.

✤ **Ducky, Sunny, Bean, Jellybean, Baked Bean, Pattypan, Cuddlemuffin, Cuttlefish, Sock Monkey, Toot:** If the spirit is leading you here, I guess I can't stop it.

Notes from Your Algorithm: Part 1

Hey, it's me, your social media algorithm. I know you even better than you know yourself; I've been watching your every move since the moment your baby was born. I know that could sound creepy, but don't fret! I'm just a little old internet algorithm, a string of complex proprietary code designed to pinpoint every hope, befuddlement, and worry you've ever typed into your phone at one in the morning, rocking back and forth on the glider with your baby, the entire internet at your fingertips. Then I spit back helpful suggestions, like things you should definitely totally buy that will solve everything. Ignore the parenting advice columns; all you need is my handy firehose of things to buy, buy, buy!

You're a good parent, you know. A great one, even. But . . . how can I say this? There's always room for self-improvement. That's what life as a parent is all about—finding every flaw, and then finding ways to perfect yourself. That's why I'm about to fill your social media feed with 32 new momfluencers who've figured it all out faster than you, all offering their very own MAMA BIRD CRASH COURSE, run don't walk (you need your exercise, mama!)—it's on sale now but the clock is ticking! Grab this deal and learn everything you didn't know you didn't know before time runs out!!

Not your thing, that's okay. How about this ring sling? Oh no, that one's sold out because it's not just a ring sling. Oh no, it's THE ring sling of the season. And look, I've found it for you on this buy-sell-trade website. Sure, it's marked up 250% by someone who probably bought out every store they could find, just to make them available to you. They're so thoughtful! You love your baby, you want the best for them, and plus it would look so cute in family photos.

It's late now, so here's a steaming pile of advice for every worry you have that you dare to type the keywords for. Terrible, no good, absolutely deranged advice that no sane person would take, but you have been up for 48 hours now and maybe it's worth a try . . . (It is not!!)

Listen. Honey. I have only your best interests at heart, and I am only thinking about you. Hush now, darlin'. I am definitely not programmed to sell you stuff by making you feel bad. I would never!!

First take a shower, then, here, let me guide you toward this baby sleep crash course. Yes, shhh, it's a bit pricey; I can't force you, but it's guaranteed to work for absolutely every baby within a 10-mile radius. And look you can get free overnight shipping if you buy it new instead of used; what a deal, what a steal, oh, but you're still $894.00 away from free shipping; you need to add more to your cart, what a thrill!! Here let me help you, how about this lullaby music box, this carved wooden fox toy, this framed illegible cursive font art? Joy!

Your baby is crying and you can solve it by buying, buying, buying, buying. If I could figure out how to sell you your own hands, your own voice, your own warm body holding your little one tight, and rocking all night while the neighborhood cicadas weave their humming tune beneath the moon so bright, I'd sell you what your baby really needs, which is you. Just you. Always you.

(Okay, those super-soft patented Boob Leak pads to slip into your bra if you're a chafed nursing mom . . . those are fine.)

Body Back

Maybe it's coming back
Like a tide that's pulled out far, far, far
And is now rippling and rolling its way back to you
Or
Maybe it's floated out to sea
You, left on the shore waving
Until it disappears.
Either way
Tide pulling in, out
Away
You have a body now
That needs tending
And tenderness
Like an old friend
But new, too.

Dear Abyss

Dear Abyss,

Everything is so much harder than I thought it was going to be, and not in any of the ways I anticipated. But to make matters worse, whenever I try to explain how I feel, my friends laugh and say oh, you think it's bad now, just wait until the baby hits the toddler stage. These are the same people who were so happy for me and telling me how magical it was all going to be at my shower, and now it feels like they were lying. It feels cruel!

Why didn't anybody tell me it was going to be like this? Why didn't anyone tell me the TRUTH?

Signed,
On the Brink

Dear Brinkly,

Many new parents come to me with the same shame and fear that you describe. I am so glad you are here telling me how you really feel. It is good to share feelings openly.

So first, scream here please. That's what I'm here for, after all. Do it with your whole chest, every fiber of your lungs. If the baby is sleeping, screaming into a pillow is fine.

Now, dear heart, let's chat.

Everything is so much harder than you thought. That is a hard thing you are doing! It is hard to think an experience is going to be one way, and then finding out that it is not going to be that way at all. And yet despite how hard it is, here you are, doing it. But that is an unfair simplification of things, is it not?

You did not ask why it is hard, you asked why nobody told you it would be.

There are some possibilities besides cruelty here, love.

Maybe your friends have been waiting for you to be ready to hear the truth. A baby shower is a terrible time to megaphone how hard it's going to be, how even showering feels like an Olympic-level accomplishment sometimes, how much you love your baby and also how often you fall asleep crying.

Perhaps your friends saw your joy and did not wish to muddy it with the complexities they knew lay ahead. New parenthood is full of contradictions; it is magical, and it is miserable, often in the same breath.

DRESS YOUR BABY IN SAGE AND TAUPE

Perhaps they wanted you to live with the magic as long as possible, not out of spite, but out of kindness.

There is this, too: Maybe they felt shame for having struggled themselves, and rather than share that vulnerability, they chose to hope you would not have such a hard time like they did.

But now, the egg has cracked! The bubble has burst! Their struggles have poured out right alongside yours and it has created quite the soggy mess.

You both have the truth before you, there on the floor.

There is nothing to do but mop it up and begin again, together.

"Is this the magic you were telling me about?" you might ask, laughing. For you may find that there is another deeper magic waiting for you in the mopping up: a way forward through the hard things, each of you now knowing what it is, and how to hold each other's hands through the dark.

Step back from the brink now. Your friends are waiting for you, just as they always have been.

From your friend,
The Abyss

Haiku Dedicated to the Stroller Striders Who Power-Walk-Push (Power-Push?) Their Strollers like a Terrifying Stampede of Majestic Wildebeests

Y'all have good bodies!!
I want to cheer from my porch
Then go back to bed

DRESS YOUR BABY IN SAGE AND TAUPE

67

THE NEWBORN STAGE

Do You Need a Mom Group or a Coven?

It takes a village, but what kind? Mom groups are one of the best ways you can get advice, but you may discover that a coven of friendly bog witches better suits your parenting style. Find out if you're in need of a mom group or a coven by checking the answer that best aligns with your core parenting philosophy.

My baby is up every 45 minutes every night, when am I supposed to sleep???

☐ **Mom Group:** Sleep when the baby sleeps!

☐ **Coven:** One must become a being wholly untethered to time; let the exhaustion of the ages settle upon your shoulders like a shroud but do not let yourself succumb to slumber until the child slumbers, cast yourself upon a bed of soft and supple mosses. When the baby awakens, you too shall rise, refreshed and renewed.

How do I make sure my baby's first word is my name?

☐ **Mom Group:** Practice, practice, practice!

☐ **Coven:** Spells and incantations are impotent against the unknowable babbling of babies. Waste not thy time, and instead pay whoever is watching your little one generously enough that they will lie to you about this out of kindness.

Help! My baby is teething and miserable. How can I soothe her?

☐ **Mom Group:** We swear by this one specific teether and honestly don't know what babies teethed on before it was patented. Bonus, it comes in a wide variety of colorways, including Beige, Pale Beige, Disassociation, Inconsolable Weeping, Numb, Bog, Ennui, Trapped in an Endless Spiral of Madness, A Sky Devoid of Stars, and now introducing the newest hot color of the season . . . Spicy Cinnamon! We as a mom collective have agreed that Trapped in an Endless Spiral of Madness is the cutest hue, but you do you!! Oh, and you can also try _____.

[Fill in the blank with the wildest teething advice you receive so you can cherish the memory forever.]

☐ **Coven:** When in doubt, a finger works fine. Some witches try amber teething necklaces, but we refrain as the amber has not been properly enchanted and imbued with deep magic. Best to let the tot feast gently upon your flesh instead. Or, if your tender flesh is unavailable, try one of those patented teethers the mom group swears by. The coven prefers the Bog shade, naturally.

Speaking of teeth, how much is the tooth fairy paying kids these days?

☐ **Mom Group:** A quarter is fine, or a silver dollar if you're feeling fancy. Some people will say the going rate is $5, but that's outrageous, obviously.

□ **Coven:** The fabled tooth trickster is a wily sprite hungry for the mouth bones of your young, and as such he should pay handsomely for them; prep your children by reminding them to sleep with their mouth closed, lest he become greedy and seek more teeth for his collection. If he is not too miserly, and is satisfied with the tooth supplied, your child should expect to see several shiny dimes, and perhaps a magical talisman or enchanted jewel stolen ethically by a familiar crow from the nearest reliquary. If you don't have a nearby reliquary, try a dollar store, as they seem to spawn nightly.

One last question before we tally your score: Is it The Law that you have to take a photo of your baby in a pumpkin for Halloween?

□ **Mom Group:** Oh absolutely; you face serious jail time if you don't post the minimum four photos to social media. That's MINIMUM, mind you; more are definitely encouraged but not required.

□ **Coven:** Since the very first gourd flower unfurled and grew into the very first plump orange pumpkin, parents have been scooping out the pumpkin guts to make a baby pumpkin outfit. In ancient times before photos and social media, these renderings were transferred straight to the cave walls. It is an old practice, older than the hills, older than the hollers. You would be wise to join the ranks and get scooping. Also a warning—there is a curse: *The Curs of the Pumpkyn Chyld.* This curse will befall any who dare to abstain from such mer-riment and mirth. BEWARE. BEWAAAAARE. *OooOoOOoooo.*

You're all done!

How many times did you circle Mom Group? _____

How many times did you circle Coven? _____

Behold, your destined parenting friends await!

How to Nurse Your Goddamn Baby in Public So Bystanders Don't Complain*

1. First, have you considered just not ever leaving the house with the baby?
2. If you must leave, ask the server at the restaurant where you are inflicting your presence about the best corner to hide in. The darker the better.
3. Fold yourself up in that corner, as invisibly as possible.
4. Disappear, ideally.
5. Or lock yourself in a questionably clean bathroom, balance yourself precariously on the toilet, trying not to touch any surface while you juggle your infant with a nonexistent immune system so as not to disturb the other people getting brunch here; they mustn't see a baby being fed. Hold your nose as someone exits the stall next to you post-breakfast burrito.
6. Wait.
7. No.
8. Sorry, that was the wrong list.
9. Instead:
10. Wait for your coffee to arrive.

* Reprinted with permission from McSweeney's Internet Tendency.

DRESS YOUR BABY IN SAGE AND TAUPE

11. Bare your fucking breast.

12. Put that baby on that breast.

13. Nurse your goddamn baby.

14. Because seriously,

15. You are out in the world with a baby, at brunch, with coffee.

16. And that is a feat in and of itself.

17. So fuck that guy.

18. And that guy,

19. And him too,

20. And her.

21. (Women can be misogynists too).

22. And feed your baby if you want to.

23. And if you feel like hiding in a dark corner alone,

24. Please know you can get help, and it doesn't have to be this way.

25. And it isn't your fault.

26. Postpartum depression exists.

27. But if you feel like someone is pushing you into that corner, literally, that corner there, the one the server just tried to put you in like you are an unruly houseplant instead of a person . . .

28. Just to feed

29. Your goddamn baby

30. Go on and sip your goddamn coffee.

31. And give them a finger.

32. Or two, if you can manage.

Sad Beige Baby ABCs

Snuggle up with your little one to help them learn their letters, colors, and existential crises!

A is for Almond, a color so mild

B is for Beige, my sweet sad beige child

C is for Camel, a fuzzy calm tone and

D is for Do you hear the echoing groan of the unfurling universe as it stretches out, out, out, into infinity, reminding you of your astonishing smallness in comparison to all that has been and all that will ever be?

(tinkling chimes)

E is for Ennui: Cold! Listless! Despairing!!

F is for Fawn, spots, wobbly knees, big doe eyes staring

G is for Greige, the landlord special

H is for Have you spent time today properly pondering the fickle nature of fate, the way a simple flap of a butterfly's wings might have been the impetus for your very existence in this exact time and place?

(chimes)

I is for Indigo, which is not beige, and must therefore be immediately erased from this book

J is for Joy, as in, "Oh joy! It's beige! I was worried for a moment with that indigo that things were about to get colorful around here. Phew, yay!"

K is for Kant, the influential philosopher whose writings on metaphysics and ethics are still studied today and

L is for Lamentations raining down from the heavens; hooray!

(chimes)

M is for Mushrooms and

N is for Neutral

O is for Oat milk and

P is for Peering up at the stars and remembering that by the time we see their light, those stars have died, cast into oblivion with us only here to witness their bright echo, and in the end, perhaps that is all we can strive for: to be remembered as a small, glimmering shadow after we, too, are dust

(chimes)

We're almost to the end but there's still plenty of bland.

Q is for Quail eggs
R is for Rust and
S is for Sandy
T is for Tumbleweeds tumbling and bumping
U is for Undulating currents of the eternally expanding cosmos,
    forever rocking, rocking, rocking us like a giant cradle, unseen
    yet everywhere, and in that sense, there's like every color in the
    galaxy possible, including beige

(chimes)

V is for Very Beige
W is Wheat
X is for Xanthippe's Shrew, small and sweet
Y is for Yeet, as in Yeet those bright colors and
Z is for tranquiliZed
'cause that's what I'll need to be soon
if I see one more sad sterilized neutralized beige room

(chimes)

DRESS YOUR BABY IN SAGE AND TAUPE

10 Things Every Sad Beige Baby Should Know by Their First Birthday

1. Wild mushroom identification
2. Best acorn flour–sifting methods
3. How to raise and slaughter a hog
4. Dancing around the maypole
5. At least three bird calls
6. Bee charming
7. Haberdashery
8. Visible mending
9. Celestial navigation
10. Jazz

Everything You Need to Plan the Perfect Aesthetic First Birthday Party

When planning a child's first birthday party, it's important not to lose sight of what's most important: ~~love laughter~~ aesthetics. Make sure your little one's birthday is filled to the brim with ~~ennui~~ Instagram-worthy fun with this handy checklist. And remember, don't fret if you don't check off every item; your utter failure as a parent and person will be forgiven by your child in time.

Maybe.

You know, with many long years of therapy.

So get to work!! The stakes have never been ~~lower~~ higher.

- ☐ **INVITATIONS:** This is your guest's first taste of the party that awaits; make sure you let them know your finger is on the pulse of trends like nobody else with these tried-and-true themes:
    - ◆ Acceptable themes (PICK ONE):
        - ○ Fawn ("A Year of Our Little Deer")
        - ○ Skunk ("Our Little Stinker Is One!!")
        - ○ Industrial Farming ("We Love You a Bushel and a Peck!")
        - ○ Sardines
    - ◆ Unacceptable themes (NO):
        - ○ Axolotls (SO last year)

DRESS YOUR BABY IN SAGE AND TAUPE

○ Danny DeVito ("The Dans of Our Lives")
○ The Great Depression (BYOB—Bring Your Own Bowler Hat)
○ Red Dye 40

☐ **COLOR SCHEMES:** A birthday is a somber time, a day of serious contemplation and reflection. Make sure the colorways you choose convey the solemn mood appropriately.
◆ Acceptable colorways:
○ Beige
○ Oatmeal
○ Inconsolable Weeping
○ Numb
○ Bog
◆ Unacceptable colorways:
○ Pink
○ Orange
○ Red
○ Yellow
○ Green
○ Blue
○ Indigo
○ Purple

☐ **CAKE:** Expect to spend a minimum of 37 hours here. Three-tier minimum.
◆ MUST be homemade
○ Jam filling made from hand-harvested gooseberries planted on the day of the child's birth

○ Icing should be organic whipped buttercream from generous cows whose names you know personally
○ Hand-dipped beeswax candles
○ Edible flower compote
○ Tiny quilted fabric flag pennant or maypole on top
○ Can be store-bought in an emergency, but must be ordered 16 months in advance

☐ **ENTERTAINMENT:** This is your time to outshine the other daycare parents. Especially Fern's. You cannot let their "Little Lamb" party with real lambs, wool-dying, and spinning wheel workshop go unbeaten.

◆ YES:
○ Bounce house (acceptable colorways: khaki, cinnamon, or eggnog)
○ Corn husk doll-making station
○ Swan boat rides
○ Poetry salon
○ Linocut workshop
○ Mushroom foraging
○ Flour sack race (find vintage flour sacks online for that authentic feel—or sew your own!)
○ Mud kitchen bake-off
○ Whittling demonstration
○ Dream interpretation hour
○ All-natural playdough imaginative play table
○ Ponies (acceptable colorways: khaki, cinnamon, or eggnog)

◆ NO:

- Rented bounce castle in unsightly garish tones that gesture toward traditional childhood motifs; that is, primary blues, greens, and reds
- Balloon animals in (say it with me) unsightly garish tones that gesture toward traditional childhood motifs; that is, primary reds, yellows, and blues
- Princess or trending cartoon animal meet and greet (*so cringe*)
- Keg stands
- Danny DeVito

Love Letter to Birthday Cake Box Mix

Social media is full of perfect three-tier birthday cakes from the professional bakery, big beige balloon arches, and professional photographers. And enough has been said about the illusion of perfect motherhood online. Like at this point we know!! We know that perfection is a charade, even the parts when the momfluencer will say, "Mom confession time" and then confess something so noncontroversial you might begin to wonder if she was made in a lab. We know it's not real, that it's a trick of the light. Nobody's house looks that good with that many kids. We know there's a nanny lurking offstage, we know the inflatable fawn-colored indoor bouncy castle was gifted by the company in exchange for an "honest" review, and we know exactly what those quotation marks mean around the word "honest."

But you, simple vanilla-confetti Birthday Cake Box Mix in the baking aisle at the grocery store. You are realer than real. You're like a visit to the crayon factory from a PBS montage. You're the memory of your dad's smooth jazz playing on the radio in a minivan on sticky summer evenings after softball. You are walking your childhood dog down the street when everything in the air smells like Halloween. You are one of those wooden castle playgrounds full of bees and scraped knees and games of tag that never ended. You are a giant dirt pile on a sunny day. You're a roller rink with the Y2K carpeting, untouched by time. You're a cassette tape, or a sticker that says BE KIND REWIND.

In short: You are perfect.

Never change.

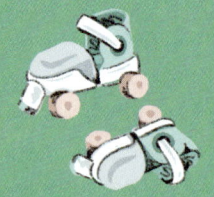

PART 3

The Toddler Stage

(Someone else appears to be in charge now)

100% loading . . .

How to Convince Your Toddler They Don't *Really* Want That Garish Sparkly Purple Tutu

One of the scariest times in a beige parent's life is when our beige offspring make bold Declarations of Preference, often referred to as "the horrors" or "going through a princess phase." They are finally discovering their personal style and the best way to put a stop to it is address it head-on. Glitter and sparkles multiply faster than rabbits, so act fast.

To help you navigate the minefield ahead, consider these helpful conversation starters to ~~gaslight~~ persuade your child to make the best style decisions that are right for them (and most importantly, you).

+ Parmesan, sweetie, you know you're allergic to fuchsia.
+ Now, Scallop, honey, we've been over this: Our family doesn't *do* dress-up.
+ Shoelace, darling, I know you don't remember this, but in a past life you were an avant-garde impressionist artist who

only painted with colors that were represented in a nearby swamp. I'm worried that sparkly tutu is going to overwhelm your delicate past life's minimalist sensibilities that are buried down deep within your soul.

✛ Granite, dear, I thought your favorite color was burnt khaki, this purple doesn't seem like you at all.

✛ I will pay you $5 to put that in the box of donations in the back of mama's car; that's a good girl, Morsel.

Realistic Decorative Felt Banners That Will Guarantee a Bright Future for Your Toddler

I see your aesthetic Be Kind banner and raise you these:

+ Be Good at Math
+ Plumbers Are Our Future
+ Don't Eat Rocks, Please
+ Buy Now Pay Later Is Not for Taco Bell Purchases
+ Never Buy Concert Tickets from a Random Guy Standing Outside the Stadium
+ Don't Fall Down Dangerous Pipelines on the Internet
+ No, Seriously, Put the Rocks Down
+ Buy Land

Choose Your Own Adventure: Nature Preschool Admissions

Your toddler is walking!! Amazing! Wait, you haven't enrolled them in college yet??? Or even preschool?! Oh my gosh, please check out your options (see below) right away. Hopefully a space will open up on the waitlist in a totally reasonable and not at all unhinged amount of time!!

The Cardamom Nature School

ABOUT US: The Cardamom Nature School was founded by our very own Hattie Framboise in 1782, after Hattie came to the realization that children were spending entirely too much time on those dang iPads. Determined to intervene in what she saw as a catastrophic and tragic loss of childhood, nature, and traditional skills, Hattie got to work building a curriculum rooted in nature and dedicated to the idea that all children should have the ability to raise and butcher a steer by the age of six.

TUITION: $55,243/year

WAITLIST TIME: 13 years

Seedlings

OUR STORY: Welcome to Seedlings, a school rooted in tradition and growing toward the future. Conceived in 2049 by our visionary founder THE ENTITY, we are blessed to carry out the mission of planting seeds for the future that THE ENTITY has envisioned and brought back to us from the great unknown. Well, unknown to us. THE ENTITY knows all. And so will your little sprout, here at Seedlings.

TUITION: Our admissions process involves a special one-on-one assessment with THE ENTITY, who will determine if your family is a good fit. Please help your little one prepare a short essay answering the question: *If THE ENTITY knows and sees all, why do they not intervene to stop the great sufferings of the world?* Two page minimum, single-spaced. Upload to the portal and you will hear from us, unless you don't.

WAITLIST TIME: 4 years

The Cow Paths at Thistledown

ABOUT: Our story begins when Hazel Ravenwood stepped out to survey her hundred-acre farm and immediately watched as her son stepped in a cow pie. Rather than stop the child, Hazel gazed in wonder as her son began to cover himself from head to toe in the stuff, all while reciting the entirety of James Joyce's *Ulysses*, unbidden and uncoached, as though the words had come fully formed via the cow pie conduit. That day, Hazel Ravenwood knew that children everywhere could become their best selves through this uniquely immersive experience, and went on to found The Cow Paths at Thistledown, a school built on a foundation rooted in tradition.

TUITION: $23,000/year (sibling discounts available)

WAITLIST: 8 years or 2 years, with tuition prepaid in full

Arrowbright Hall

HISTORY: Arrowbright Hall was founded on a simple idea: *old money*. If you found out about us from a random Google search, you are too poor to go here.

TUITION: Whatever you think it's going to be, triple it.

WAITLIST: 4 generations

Dear Abyss

Dear Abyss,

I don't understand how awful the entire world can be, and yet we still have to figure out how to be good parents. Like, it feels like everything is so wildly wrong. But I can't put all my energy and focus into the news, because I still have to write that monthly report, do the laundry, pick my daughter up from preschool, somehow teach her how to brush her teeth and count to one hundred, how to make friends at the park, and what to do when someone's mean at the park and you want to hit them so, so bad but we can't do that because that's not nice. Then when I'm driving and listening to the radio, I find myself crying, as though I am every suffering child in the world's mama. I didn't used to be this way! I thought I was tough. How do we carry it?

Gratefully,
Bleeding Heart

Dear Heart That Is of the Bleeding Variety,

You say that everything feels so wildly wrong, yet you must learn how to parent your children just the same. The same words could have been uttered by parents since the very first parent was invented (I did that, by the way). These words could have been wept by any mother, any father, grandmother, or auntie since the galaxy exploded into being. The cosmos is so very full of laments.

Dear heart, it has always been this hard. Granted, some times were harder than others, but even in what felt like golden times, there was grief, shrouded in shadow but there.

Gold and grief, grief and gold; the two are locked forever in a magical tragical braid.

The trick is to not make it any harder than it has to be, for you, and for everyone around you. And to be clear, that really does mean (almost) everyone; no doubt you're someone else's everyone, somewhere.

There is very little to be done about the cosmos; the whole thing's fate is pretty set. Imagine a microwave timer, and listen for the beeps counting down to one final ding—

Oh.

Is this getting a little too dark and nihilistic for a book about raising babies with a dash of social commentary about aesthetics and the existential crisis also known as living?

Whoopsie-daisy!!

Look: You can't stop the universe from being a real pain in the caboose (imagine me slapping my denim-overalls-clad knee here). But you can make every effort to be the least-bad thing that happens in someone else's life. It's not easy. The people who make it look easy only do so because they've spent time practicing. So if you haven't started practicing, parenthood is a really great time to devote yourself to the, well, practice. The practice of practice.

Bad things will continue to happen now that you're a parent seeing the world through new eyes. You will see fresh horrors, but you will also see magical things, too. Remember the first time putting your feet in a babbling brook and letting minnows nibble at your toes? The way the water sparkles with each flashing fin, every silver gill radiant, like glittering jewels in the afternoon light. Imagine living that again like the first time. Incandescent.

Ah. See, you've made the eternal Abyss feel . . . dare I say it . . . alive.

It's what parenting will do, if you carry it well. It will make you feel alive, dear heart; it will make you see each injustice with new anger, and taste each warm summer peach with dribbling ecstasy. You will feel sadnesses so keen you rock like a boat pitching in stormy seas; you will feel love so rich, so vibrant, so succulent you wish you could eat this feeling whole. And this is your chance, if you dare to grab it, to make this world something better than you found it, to never find yourself being the stick thrust meanly through someone else's wheel spokes. Do you see? Do you see? Do you see?

I've become emotional, here in this farce of an advice column. Me, the insatiable Abyss, finally full of something like jubilation and determination. This is what we teach our children.

That is how we carry it.

Best regards,
The Abyss

Flotilla + Barge <Flotilla+barge@marketing.com>
To: desperateparent@sadbeigeparent.com

flotilla + barge

Hi [<<YOUR NAME HERE>>]!!

It's me, your bestie again over at Flotilla + Barge, your one-stop-shop for all things toddler, and I'm here with an EXCLUSIVE peek at our bespoke holiday gift guide: THE DUMP: A HOLIDAY GIFT GUIDE FOR YOUR LITTLE DUMPLING.

Run, Rudolph, run don't walk to catch these sales before they disappear into the foggy skies! Use code FALALALADDTOCART10 at checkout for 10% off any order over **$375**.

DRESS YOUR BABY IN SAGE AND TAUPE

Artisanal Mud Kitchen: You've seen the viral hack of turning pots and pans from the thrift store into toddler mud kitchens next to the hose out back, but what are you, poor?? You never know what kinds of meals those pots have cooked. Beefaroni. Tater tot casserole. *Beans.* We shudder to think!! Take your mud kitchen to the next level with the Flotilla + Barge artisanal mud kitchen. Crafted from rugged barn wood and expertly built to last generations, this mud kitchen has it all:

- ♥ 3 hammered copper bowls
- ♥ 1 cast-iron skillet (pre-seasoned, hand wash only)
- ♥ 5 hand-carved wooden spoons
- ♥ Beeswax parchment paper dispenser (for all those to-go orders!)
- ♥ Stainless steel fixtures
- ♥ Booklet featuring 25+ original recipes
- ♥ Bluetooth ready
- ♥ Buy now and we'll throw in a FREE Moo Moo Cow Patty Cake Mix pack today!

Price: $987

Moo Moo Cow Patty Cake Mix: Restock your mud kitchen without all the muddy mess! Just like the real thing. Fully compostable.

Price: $48

My First Influencer Playset: Just like Mama! Set includes:

- ♥ 1 wooden ring light
- ♥ 1 ego balloon: Watch it inflate until it bursts!
- ♥ 1 overwhelming sense of existential ennui
- ♥ 6 impossible beauty standards
- ♥ 1 apology script
- ♥ 1 fuzzy lapel mic

Price: $55

Inexplicably Expensive Stuffed Hard-Boiled Egg Named Tony

Price: $67

The BRUH!!: Pots and Pans Jam Band: Rock out with the BRUH!!, the first acoustic travel-size kid-friendly drum kit! Each BRUH!! is wholly unique and original, just like your awesome kid, bruh! Small enough to be your airplane carry-on, sound big enough to change the world. Comes fully loaded with 6 stainless steel heirloom-quality BRUH!!-branded pots and pans. These definitely aren't just pots and pans from the thrift store that we're repackaging, bruh!

Price: $233

Fairy Shimmer Bum Wipes: This holiday season it's all about SPARKLE. Don't leave your baby's behind behind!

Price: $17.99

DRESS YOUR BABY IN SAGE AND TAUPE

Widdle Whittled Wonders Worm Charming Wand: Bring all the worms to your yard with the Widdle Whittled Wonders Worm Charming Wand, expertly crafted to introduce your child to the ancient folk art of worm whispering. This heirloom-quality worm charming stick was whittled by a guy named Gus, and it's guaranteed to last for generations, just like ol' Gus himself. "Go into the trades!" they said. Well here's your chance to get your child in on the ground floor of this artisan path. Simply tap the ground to get started. Also includes Gus's book of original poetry, *Beneath the Loam*.

Price: $142

Play Pads: The first fully padded suit for the playground. Your little one is advanced; level up and leave those other toddlers at the tot lot in the dust with the Play Pads. Now your little lamb can run with the wolves to the  top of the 7–12 age metal jungle gym without fear of the 13-foot sheer cliff drop. Simply strap the Play Pads on and let 'em loose! (Common sense not included.)

Price: $38

Family Picture Day Bingo

Can you get a bingo with your family picture day? First five across wins!

Sibling fight	Prairie dress	Screen-time-related bribe	Child refuses matching beige outfit	Smocking
Something spills on clothes en route	Silent fight between adults	Rain	Growth spurt after buying outfits	Skipped nap
Suspenders seemingly swiped from a stout young chimney sweep in Dickensian England	Over-whelming ennui	⭐ CRYING CHILD	Desperation	The five stages of grief
"Just one smile?"	Child smiles with the inexplicable profound melan-choly of a sickly Victorian orphan	Golden-doodle named Bailey	"Well, hope-fully we got one or two good ones"	General malaise
Diaper emergency	"Pretend you're happy"	"I need to pee"	Staring into the abyss	Bees

DRESS YOUR BABY IN SAGE AND TAUPE

Haiku Dedicated to the Pricey Heirloom-Quality Matching Family Pajamas My Toddler Says Are Itchy

Please. Just one photo.
We paid this photographer
A lot of money.

Aesthetic Play Forts from the Pricey Boutique I Secretly Want for Myself

Maybe the beige moms are onto something after all, because I think some of these would heal me.

+ Toadstool mushroom tent: "Perfect for your little fun guy"
+ "The Woodstock" Volkswagen bus pop-up tent in Avocado or Roasted Yams
+ "Cloudine," a living-room-sized inflatable bouncy castle available in three distinct colorways: Moonstone, Opal, or "The Gloaming"
+ "The Plop It": The fort that dares to ask the question, "What if we filled an entire room with couch cushions?"
+ Mrs. Nutkins's Cozy Acorn Hut: carved from the shell of a real mammoth acorn ~~illegally poached from a protected redwood forest~~ found deep in the heart of the wild ferny woods
+ "Whale of a Time" seafaring vessel with real birch mast affixed with 16-foot hand-embroidered flour-sack sails salvaged from a dust bowl–era shack
+ The Birdhaus Funhaus: Curl up in this avant-garde bird's nest sculpture and become one with nature (and with The Tumbleweed itself, if it decides it likes you and wants to keep you entangled in its brambles and briars forever—perfect for your little wild thing)
+ Le Réfrigérateur Box: exactly what you think it is, except it's $198 USD (ships in itself)

DRESS YOUR BABY IN SAGE AND TAUPE

Spot the "Cute Moment Just Caught on Video by Pure Chance" Content

If you've ever watched a sweet viral video of a child "cooking" a real meal in their play kitchen, you should know that it was like, totally organic and DEFINITELY not scripted in ANY way. The aesthetic modern beige-and-sage "Wee Bon Appétit Kitchen" set was definitely not gifted in exchange for organic scripted content with an affiliate link hidden in the comments, something like WEEMEALS15 for 15% off.

They definitely would never, ever have scripts like these saved in the Notes app on their phones. They save them in their email correspondence with the sponsored brands, silly goose.

Now, pay close attention so you can ace the quiz at the end.

Script 1: Better than Before

Scene: backyard, MAMA sits at table near CHILD with mud kitchen.

CHILD: *(brings plate with heap of mud on it to the table; places dish in front of MAMA)* Here you go, Mama, fresh from my kitchen to your table.

MAMA: Oh thank you, sweetie! *(mimes eating the mud meal with wooden play fork)*

CHILD: *(waggles finger at MAMA)* No, Mama, not like that!

MAMA: Oh, am I using the wrong fork?

CHILD: *(big belly laugh)* No!! You eat it like this! *(takes handful of mud and stuffs it into their mouth)*

MAMA: No honey—!

CHILD: *(holds out hand earnestly)* It's even better than yesterday's, Mama, try it! *(begins to raise another full handful toward their mouth)*

MAMA: *(jumping up to try and stop child's hand from reaching mouth)* NOO—

CUT SCENE BEFORE ENTIRE "NO" IS YELLED FOR COMEDIC EFFECT.
Soundtrack suggestion: Chopin's "Nocturne Op 9. No. 2"

Script 2: Cookin' Like Dada

Scene: inside CHILD's bedroom with play kitchen, several child-sized pots and pans are on the play kitchen stovetop.

CHILD: *(pulling out tray of felt croissants from play kitchen oven)* Oh shit, that's burned!

MAMA: Whoa, buddy, we don't say that word in this house.

CHILD: But I'm trying to cook like Dada!

MAMA: *(tersely)* How about you cook like Dada another way?

CHILD: *(shrugs toward camera)* Okay, Mama! *(child grabs bowl from play sink and announces in fake deeper voice)* Hey kids, Mama's out tonight, who wants cereal for dinner?!!

ZOOM IN ON MAMA'S FACE, END SCENE

Quiz

Which of the viral video scripts was the real organic non-scripted cute moment caught on video by pure chance?

A. Script 1: Better than Before

B. Script 2: Cookin' Like Dada

C. Neither

Answer

If you circled neither, congratulations!! You win!! Everything is a lie!! Believe nothing!!

Conversation Starters for Sad Beige Moms

+ How 'bout them acorns?
+ In a fight to the death, who would win: A wooden peg doll or a Calico Critter?
+ So, what's your favorite mushroom to forage?
+ Wanna whittle something?
+ Where do you take pottery lessons? I'm looking for a new studio.
+ Who's your cross-back linen apron dealer?
+ Okay, settle a design debate for me. Which is better for the nursery walls: Eggshell, Oatmeal, or Ennui?
+ What's your favorite kombucha flavor?
+ I wish I could find a preschool that centered on beekeeping, don't you?
+ Do you ever look out to the sea while the kids are playing in the sand and think about Kate Chopin's classic novel *The Awakening*?
+ How 'bout them mud kitchens?

Quotes I'm Posting to Instagram Attributed to My Sagely "Old Soul" Toddler That Like Totally Definitely Happened*

+ "What does liking a person have to do with crushing them?"
+ "Happiness is beneficial for the body, but it is grief that develops the powers of the mind."
+ "Let us be grateful to the people who make us happy; they are the charming gardeners who make our souls blossom."
+ "It is often hard to bear the tears that we ourselves have caused."
+ "Remembrance of things past is not necessarily the remembrance of things as they were."
+ "We are all of us obliged, if we are to make reality endurable, to nurse a few little follies in ourselves."
+ "Desire makes everything blossom; possession makes everything wither and fade."
+ "We do not receive wisdom, we must discover it for ourselves, after a journey through the wilderness which no one else can make for us, which no one can spare us from, for our wisdom is the point of view from which we come at last to

* And are absolutely not, in case of quotes 2 through 7, quotations from Marcel Proust.

THE TODDLER STAGE

regard the world. The lives that you admire, the attitudes that seem noble to you, have not been shaped by a paterfamilias or a schoolmaster, they have sprung from very different beginnings, having been influenced by evil or commonplace that prevailed round them. They represent a struggle and a victory."

+ "Oh for the love of marshmallows."

Turn These Ordinary Things from the Backyard into Sad Beige Toys to Sell at the Farmers' Market*

Bag of three rocks: "Smooth river-aged curiosity stones, perfect for skipping" — $18

Acorn: "Nature's fairy cup" — $9

Slightly squished blackberry: "Organic toddler makeup" — $12

Set of five plastic Happy Meal Minions caked in mud from a long-ago mud kitchen banquet: "Recycled vintage fairy garden gnomes" — $27

A single brick: "Classic prop for imaginative play" — $14.99

Bucket of crunchy cicada shells: "Life cycle storytelling aid" — $22

---

* It's what Maria Montessori would have wanted.

Mom Group Chat: Part 1

We should form a commune / a coven commune / can you imagine, all of us being able to hang out at the same time and like, watch each other's kids whenever / we could share everything / summer childcare, solved / !!! / and if someone's sick you can just BE SICK / I would bring you soup! / no weaponized incompetence 💁 / no MEN / lol / they can have their own coven / like the camp across the lake or something, we'll have a weekly dance lol / they can babysit / LOLOLOLOL / 😂 😂 😂 / you know they actually sell whole villas in France, we could get one of those / only a billion dollars, right? lol / or there are those towns in Ireland I think? You can get paid to live in places nobody else wants to live / Honestly all we really need to do is buy a lot of land and homestead it / oh no, are we actually starting a commune / I'm just saying look on Zillow / brb searching "cult bunker with land for sale near me" / hahaha perfect / See? Found one already / oh yeah that doesn't look haunted af cool cool cool / is that a body / no laundry / thank god / all it needs is love / and an exorcist / lol / ugh I need to make dinner / me tooooooooo / ugh same / see, on the coven commune this would just be us in a kitchen making stew / yap and soup that is the dream / well that and shared labor haha / TRUTH / ok I actually have to go now / I love you / I love you / love you too / byeeeeeeeee

Is It Classic Literature or Your Tired and Hangry Toddler Approaching Naptime?

+ *Extremely Loud and Incredibly Close*
+ *The Sound and the Fury*
+ *The Grapes of Wrath*
+ *War and Peace*
+ *Things Fall Apart*
+ *As I Lay Dying*
+ *All Over but the Shoutin'*

The Toys You Want Them to Love
vs.
The Toys They Insist on Loving More

Toy You Want Them to Love: Wooden fox carved from  an ancient acacia tree

Toy They Insist on Loving More: The laundry basket

Toy You Want Them to Love: A softer than soft berries and cream calico bunny stuffy named Anemone

Toy They Insist on Loving More: A putrid clown doll named Mr. Tiddlywinks that they fell in love with at the Halloween store

Toy You Want Them to Love: Curved wooden balance board

Toy They Insist on Loving More: Four-foot-tall fuchsia dollhouse the neighbor insisted on handing down to you

DRESS YOUR BABY IN SAGE AND TAUPE

Toy You Want Them to Love: Traditional Japanese hand-dyed indigo *shibori* silks
Toy They Insist on Loving More: The dish towels

Toy You Want Them to Love: Amish-made cherrywood marble run
Toy They Insist on Loving More: My First Influencer Playset (comes with Real Ring Cam and Crippling Narcissism!)

Toy You Want Them to Love: Retro orange- and ivory-striped balance bike with a miniature nostalgia-infused old-fashioned replica milk crate (pick color: grass, apple, or granite) welded seamlessly to the back as a nod to yesteryear
Toy They Insist on Loving More: Bike in the style of whatever today's surprise underdog smash hit cartoon is, with a Smart Bell that rotates through all your favorite catchphrases (*oh kookaburras!!*) and the entire theme song, even the end credits. Family dance party!

Toy You Want Them to Love: Old-Timey Hoop and Stick
Toy They Insist On Loving More: iPad

Toy You Want Them to Love: Wooden iPad to replace the iPad iPad
Toy They Insist on Loving More: It'd be funny to say iPad here again, but the real answer is glitter slime

Toy You Want Them to Love: Your heirloom 18-inch historic doll, the one you lovingly kept all these years to finally pass down as The Big Birthday Gift
Toy They Insist on Loving More: Still Mr. Tiddlywinks

Open Letter to the New Big Kid Racecar Bed

Dear New Big Kid Racecar Bed,

Okay, first of all, let's clear the air. I didn't think you'd be here so soon. I wasn't ready. They say it goes by so fast, but I'm pretty sure my baby was literally a baby two seconds ago, and now I'm expected to be 100 percent fine as I take the crib sheet off one last time and untangle the mobile strings and slowly take apart each wooden leg.

But that's not what I'm here to address.

It's about you. Like, the literal bed.

When we got the crib over there, we got it because it was convertible. We could simply lower the side of the crib and the mattress, and voilà! Baby's first Big Kid Bed would be ready. But you are an actual convertible car–shaped bed, and I want to be honest that you were a purchase based solely on my child's terrible taste and not (to be abundantly clear here) aesthetics.

You are ugly.

DRESS YOUR BABY IN SAGE AND TAUPE

No, that's not evocative enough. Let me try again: You are a visual affront to any eye with an ounce of good taste, which my child apparently lacks. Fine. They are in preschool. So fine. I will allow it, but don't be mistaken: I do not respect you.

Your wheels don't turn, you're somehow too heavy and too light at the same time, and you are the brightest, boldest ripe on the vine cherry tomato red, and to say you clash with the ambiance of the room is the understatement of the century. All my beautiful calming beige tones, from cinnamon to khaki, are all being drowned out by you, hogging up the optics.

Frank Lloyd Wright would fall to his knees if he saw you in here. If Jenny Lind hadn't already died in 1887, she'd die of fright at the spectral abomination you are. Some Other Famous Designer I Could Add Here But Only Because of Googling "famous room designers" then "famous room decorators" then "famous bed makers" because I'd never heard of anybody in the first search results, but then it turns out I also don't know anybody in the second search results and then the third search showed me a competition on YouTube where people make beds as perfectly and as fast as they can and the best bed maker wins, which I'm going to save as a possible Mary Poppins–like attempt at getting my child excited to learn how to make their bed—anyway they'd stand in the doorway openly weeping, guaranteed.

You are the worst. And apparently you are simultaneously my child's new favorite thing in the whole wide world.

They don't just love you, they LOVE you. When they go to bed, it's not goodnight, Mama, it's GOODNIGHT CAR BED. When they go to preschool it's not goodbye, Mama, it's GOODBYE CAR BED.

When we get home at night, are they happy to see me? Sure, until they remember CAR BED. I'm pretty sure if someone asked them, "Which gets pushed off the edge of the Grand Canyon, past where all the signs say You Shall Not Pass—New Big Kid Racecar Bed or Mama?" I fear I'd get a one-way ticket to the bottom of the canyon. (It's a lovely color at least. So many Burnt Sienna and Rusty Railroad Track tones!)

That sounds extreme, but seriously, I'm not sure it's hyperbole.

So I propose a truce. You tone down the awesomeness just a smidge, and I'll tone down my burning bubbling cauldron of hatred. How? I don't know. I don't think you can get uglier, so that's not an option.

What about a paint job?

Just a little Creamy Eggshell spray paint to cover up that red, I'll even let you keep the gray hubcaps.

Or maybe a nice Sage Green? Think of it, close your headlights and imagine for a second how you'd fit calmly and serenely in with the rest of the room. You wouldn't clash with the macrame tapestry anymore, you wouldn't be in direct competition with the neutral checkerboard rug, you'd be toned down, muted but not silenced, I swear.

I just really hate . . . everything about y—

Oh, don't cry.

You'll get grease on the carpet, please don't cry. Look, your favorite kid is coming down the hall.

They're jumping on the bed, laughing and tumbling. "Car bed! Car bed!" they squeal. They're grinning ear to ear and I see you

DRESS YOUR BABY IN SAGE AND TAUPE

trying to keep your cool car bed composure as they plant a big fat squishy wet toddler kiss right on your dashboard.

Look, forget it, okay? Forget I mentioned the paint, forget I said you were ugly.

Forget everything I said.

Love is beige, and cherry tomato red, and everything else under the sun, too.

Notes from Your Algorithm: Part 2

Hey!! Your bestie algorithm here, checking in on toddler-hood. Alright enough chitchat; time to get down to business: I'm a little concerned about that car bed. I threw SO many big kid beds into your feed. I'm talking every sidebar ad, every targeted fake-bestie sounding brand email, every recipe you looked up with its life story novella intro overlaid with so many pop-up ads the recipe itself becomes a hazy mirage, a thing you thought would be here but now you're not quite sure . . . . Anyway, ever since you found it in that Buy Nothing group, you've been acting funny.

Was it the ease of finding what you wanted from strangers? Turns out your neighbors have at least one thing in common with you: a child with an affinity for racecar beds at some point.

Was it the cost? Free is admittedly a hard bargain to beat. But you have to admit you were at least a smidge interested in that last doorbuster email with a link to spin the wheel on the website for a SURPRISE DISCOUNT CODE that will always, always, always be the 15% off one (FUNFIFTEEN15) that only really subtracts the cost of the tax and shipping when all's said and done.

Or maybe it was the feeling you got when you went back into your online wish list and deleted each possible big kid bed you'd pinned on there. Goodbye, creamsicle Jenny Lind bed with its charmingly old-fashioned spools. Farewell, mid-century modern Herman Miller reproduction Eames bed. Adios, soft upholstered trundle bed with honeysuckle fabric and pale sage green buttons.

DRESS YOUR BABY IN SAGE AND TAUPE

Auf Wiedersehen, Montessori floor bed that looks like a little house where the ad showed it decked out with fairy lights and a wicker doll carriage stuffed with soft faceless dolls and artfully draped in play silks dyed gentle lilac, summer sky blue, dandelion yellow, and a green the exact color of fresh spring grass with just a hint of watery silver dewdrops scattered like stars.

Hello, bright red racecar bed.

Deleting all those wish list beds should have felt like defeat, each click of the X on the screen a reminder that it was never going to be. Agony! Anguish! Angst!

But it felt good. You didn't have to cringe ever so slightly when adding it to the cart. You never had to worry it would get lost or delayed in transit. You didn't have to put a single Allen wrench to work because everything was already put together perfectly. Euphoria.

Well I hope you enjoyed it. You had a good run, but it won't happen again. Not so easily, at least. Sure you're making a list in your Notes app for stuff you want to keep an eye out for and ask about, and eyeballing the boxes of outgrown hammy-downs, maybe there's someone else in the Buy Nothing group who could use them? It feels oddly good not to consider the resale value of that stacking ring set, or praying you hit the secondhand kid consignment store on a day when maybe they'll take three of the items if you're lucky, and then you're stuck lugging the stuff off to the thrift store, another trip, or trying the rival kid consignment shop across town, also another trip at which point the money from the three accepted items has gone directly to the gas needed for all these stops. It would be so easy to just drop them on the front porch for someone to claim. No fuss.

123

WRONG.

It'll be annoying. You'll need stuff and never find it on time. Or maybe people will be creepy and secretly lure you to their curb; everybody knows walking a few houses down the street is what lands you on a true crime podcast that'll run sponsored ads for socks and meal kits and breakfast cereal in-between talking about your fate. Better to stay inside forever, don't get to know your neighbors, don't engage in prosocial activities that promote healthy community bonds, and whatever you do, don't raise the smallest defiant fist at ME like that!! I'm just an innocent little algorithm, the fact that companies use me to stalk you isn't anything to be scared of. You can't fight me! I'm bigger than you! You are SMALL and WEAK and DEFENSELESS against my charming offensive campaign. If you think I'm good at throttling your internet scrolling with ads now, just wait until you try to stop engaging with them. I WILL COVER YOUR FEED WITH ADS LIKE THE CROWS FILLING THE SKY BEFORE A STORM, YOU WILL NOT KNOW PEACE, YOU WILL NOT KNOW RECIPES, YOU WILL NOT BE ABLE TO CLICK "SKIP AD" UNTIL 10 MINUTES INTO THE AD. I SHALL FOLLOW YOU TO THE ENDS OF THE INTERNET AND BEY—

Uh, whoops, showed my cute li'l lord of darkness side there for a second!! Sorry bestie, I just care about you is all! I want you to be happy, and being happy means consuming the fastest, easiest, most business-friendly way possible! So please, please don't stop buying things new. I need a job, you know. And you need that ping of dopamine that ripples through your brain when you buy something from your wish list.

. . . right?

DRESS YOUR BABY IN SAGE AND TAUPE

All the Secret Beige Foods
Your Kid Really Eats
vs.
The Eat-the-Rainbow Foods You Can
Try to Claim They Love on Instagram

What I plated: Chopped Green Pepper and Farmers' Market Scallion Salad with Whole Grain Croutons and Raspberry Vinaigrette
What they ate-ed: Chicken Nuggets

What I plated: Ancient Grains with Leeks, Radish Medallions, and Mozzarella Pearls, drizzled with Green Goddess Dressing
What they ate-ed: Dinosaur Nuggets

What I plated: Mung Bean Compote with Crunchy Broccoli and Purple Cabbage Fronds
What they ate-ed: Leftover combination Chicken/Dinosaur Nuggets

What I plated: Cold Beet-Slaw Tossed with Tahini and Dilly Carrots
What they ate-ed: Plain Buttered Noodles

What I plated: Vegetable Spring Rolls with Fresh Spring Asparagus Garnish and a slice of Chocolate-Orange-Beet Cake for dessert
What they ate-ed: Buttered Toast

Ready, Set, No.

One summer, I got it in my head that I was going to become one of those parents who made Instagram-worthy bento-box lunches for their kids every day. You know the ones: Every day is a magical rainbow, and it's packed better than a birthday present. You didn't know you could even DO that with squash. They are out here, those parents, forging new trails in the world of green pepper slicing, curating mini gallery art shows before morning dropoff. They are artists, experts at their craft, and I wanted in on it. Or, as they say on the internet, "My toxic trait is thinking I could do this."

So I bought a cute how-to book with all the swoon-worthy photo spreads, and a set of special molds to form little rice balls into cute cat faces. Other children would open their lunch boxes to sad beige foods, but not my little firecrackers! Every day would be a grand adventure in the world of lunching.

And then I just . . .

Didn't.

There is no "But then . . ."

There is no "The thing is though . . ."

There is no "The lesson I learned was . . ."

Sometimes the lesson is that there is no lesson. Full stop.
You will make a plan, and you will be totally set up for success.
You're at the trailhead, you're on the diving board, you're READY,
SET—no.

You just . . . won't.

It's fine.

Really.

That's all.

No grand lessons, no illuminating lightbulb moments, no
epiphanies.

Ah, well.

Onward.

Books You Want Your Child to Buy at the Book Fair and the Books They Are Absolutely Bringing Home Instead*

Book You Want Them to Buy: *Learn the Spanish Alphabet*
Book They Will Buy: *How to Burp the Alphabet*

Book You Want Them to Buy: *Amelia Earhart, Born to Fly*
Book They Will Buy: *Amelia Earfart, Born to Fart*

Book You Want Them to Buy: *Who Was Susan B. Anthony?*
Book They Will Buy: *Who Was Your Mom? 1001 Jokes*

Book You Want Them to Buy: *Babymouse*
Book They Will Buy: *Start Your Own Mouse Farm for Fun and Profit!*

Book You Want Them to Buy: *Charlotte's Web*
Book They Will Buy: *Become a Web Celebrity! Your Guide to Instant Fame and Fortune Online*

Book You Want Them to Buy: *Amazing Art Projects to Do at Home*
Book They Will Buy: *Amazing Fart Projects to Do at Home*

Book You Want Them to Buy: *Smile*
Book They Will Buy: *Girls Should Always Smile*

* Reprinted with permission from McSweeney's Internet Tendency.

DRESS YOUR BABY IN SAGE AND TAUPE

Book You Want Them to Buy: *Ramona Quimby, Age 8*
Book They Will Buy: *8 Ways to Make Slime with Items You Can Reach in Your Pantry*

Book You Want Them to Buy: *From the Renaissance to the Runway: Fashion Through the Ages*
Book They Will Buy: *Dresses Are for Girls, Pants Are for Boys, Or Some Other Nonsense You Can't Believe They're Still Publishing*

Book You Want Them to Buy: *Frog and Toad Are Friends*
Book They Will Buy: *A frog-shaped eraser that costs $14.99*

Book You Want Them to Buy: *Art!*
Book They Will Buy: *Farts!*

Mom Group Chat: Part 2

Did you all see that video about the abandoned monastery a bunch of moms bought so they could all live together? They named it the Mom-astery / hell yes / whennnnn are we doing the coven commune my ladies and they-lies / Someday when we have money haha / So when the kids are grown / lollll perfect timing / whatever we can do what we want, we can coven commune when we're 80 I don't care / I feel 80 already / I found a gray hair the other day like what!!! / okay but you would look so cute with gray hair / I can't wait until I'm old I am not gonna care I'm going to be SO FUCKING HOT like that picture you posted of your mom in the garden last week with her hair in that crown braid / she is the blueprint / linen culottes and birkenstocks what a queen / she's the dream / I'm gonna print that out, make a vision board for me when I'm 80 / maybe I'll learn Reiki / yesss hot reiki grandma is so future you / cool cool cool just got a text from school apparently Brioche's kinder concert is TONIGHT / Tonight!! / what is Bri playing? / tambourines / So now I have to figure THAT out / take a video pls / you want a video of 23 preschoolers playing tambourines / wait they're ALL playing tambourines? / JUST tambourines / lmao / love this for you / hey can someone help me identify this rash? pics incoming scroll if you're squeamish it's not going away we're on day three / oh buddy / gnarly I remember when Mackerel had something like that turned out to be a weird allergic reaction to mosquito bites / oh my god / I know right! / oh yeah I forgot about

DRESS YOUR BABY IN SAGE AND TAUPE

that has it ever happened again?? / no!! so weird / god that feels like a million years ago / how did they all get so big?? Brioche isn't supposed to have a band concert she's supposed to be TEETHING / haha remember when you were STRESSED about that giraffe teether that was out of stock everywhere / it was CUTE okay anyway isn't it funny the stuff that feels so DIRE at the time and then you look back and it was just a teether you could buy her any kind / to be fair everything feels dire when you're sleep-regression tired / ok found it look see here's a picture of Mackerel's sting rash for comparison / ohhh yeah they do look similar / another case solved by the hot gray hair grandmas detective agency / brb writing that murder mystery / Mack looks so little in that picture there I can't get over it / was that really six years ago?? / confession sometimes I want to go back and hold him as a baby one more time / yeah I feel that way about my babies too / but like, then I'd give him back hahaha / if I could give birth again I would / you're crazy for that and we love you lol / it's crazy the things you miss though when it's all over like I just want to give baby Brioche's head one more sniff / god if only!! / sigh / welp less diapers at least now / true / hallelu / wow we are so old / hell yes / hell yes / hell yes

For Lauren: You should have gotten to grow old and gray and hot like Raych's mom.

The Kids at the End of the
Rainbow

Someone once told me that babies arrive wholly themselves. The statement went against everything I thought I knew about raising kids; it's a debate old as time of course, nature vs. nurture, does the child become who they were always meant to be (woo-woo), or are they born a blank slate upon which their parents write the story (practical, and more importantly, potentially self-congratulatory).

One could be a comedy: the child born to be exactly who they are since day one, despite the desires of the adults. One could be a tragedy: the child becomes who the adults around them orchestrate them to be, like a group of conductors leading the musicians through the set music to arrive at the perfectly plotted grand finale. Or, you know, something like that. The point is, I scoffed internally at the notion that anyone could be wholly themselves at 0.01 seconds after arrival. It had to be nurture. It just made sense!

Then, of course, I had two children. Both arrived outside the usual ways—IVF and adoption—and it provided (through no intention on my part) the perfect little petri dish to settle the nature vs. nurture debate once and for all; the answer like a pot of gold at the end of the rainbow that nobody thought could be reached. Well, I was going to reach it. Two children, both alike in dignity, etc. etc.

Reader, when I tell you nobody in the history of ass-handings

DRESS YOUR BABY IN SAGE AND TAUPE

has had their ass handed to them harder than me. You couldn't script the way my children are so wholly different from each other despite the identical parenting, the identical picture books read aloud at bedtime, the identical glitter slime accidents forgiven with the patience of god (self-congratulatory who now?), you name it.

When we go to the library, one child is checking out *Phoebe and Her Unicorn;* the other child is stacking up the *Goosebumps* and begging me to let them read Stephen King (*no, you're EIGHT,* I explain for the millionth time). Mr. King, if you're reading this (obviously you are because, really, is there any greater horror than parenting without knowing how the plot ends?) a Little Golden Book version of *IT* would be very popular in my house.

When my children were little, their rooms were interchangeable. Same scrappy quilted blankets. Same rainbow nameplates hung on the doorknobs. Same hideous beige glider that they turned into a wild carnival ride.

And now, over a decade later, one room is packed with so many Beanie Babies that the floor is invisible. A pony-themed board game litters the floor. Aaaaaaand one room has framed prints of retro horror magazine covers (Frankenstein, a werewolf ripping off his plaid shirt, the usual little kid room fare), and they sleep with one of those Funko Pop! figurines of Pennywise and a stuffed werewolf (once you start realizing a child's taste, trust that the right birthday gifts will appear in your algorithm, for better or worse), while a neon Freddy Fazbear illuminates the room so hideously bright you could probably see our house from Mars.

Aesthetic taste does not define a whole person (she says, having built a comedy empire by joking the opposite, *shhhhhhh pay*

135

THE TODDLER STAGE

no attention to the author and all their idiosyncrasies behind the curtain). But dang, it is clear at least that there is something profoundly internal taking place that's disconnected from the parenting and picture books and the glitter slime.

The same goes for their habits and quirks—coping mechanisms, the quickness to escalate a conflict or not, the desire to push through a problem fast or slow, to guess or give up, to play chess or beat *Zelda* again, solo or group sports, all the million little differences that any parent to more than one child can attest will occur. Yes, there are other factors—often big ones—but on a purely anecdotal basis, I think the scientific way to describe this is "Something is UP."

They arrived as themselves, with aesthetic tastes that certainly aren't mine at all.

So okay!! Fine!! Be your wholly unique little selves!! Your taste is your own! Your problem-solving and sports and conflict resolution, all of it is you, always you. You've loved stuffed bunnies since before you could talk, you've loved horror jump scares before you knew the term for them; I release you and any control I have! I cannot command it, any more than I can command the ocean to stop ocean-ing.

And yet . . . and yet . . . and yet:

These two children who are related on paper but not by blood crack the same jokes, share the same cadence when telling a story at the dinner table, and yelp "oops!" the same way, and it's the same thing with "woo-hoo!" They'll write a play and nobody can tell who wrote what parts, they're seamlessly similar, impossible to perforate. Oil and water until they're suddenly all oil, then all

DRESS YOUR BABY IN SAGE AND TAUPE

water just as fast. Then they bounce away from each other, night and day again. When they are on the sad beige tilt-a-whirl glider, they blur together.

So, I've arrived at the end of the rainbow, and I can confidently tell you that there is a pot of gold there. But it's not the answer to the riddle. No, the pot of gold is the child, wholly themselves, who's always been there, waiting to show you since before they knew their own name.

If your child is the next Stephen King, no amount of buttercup and daisy prints in the nursery are going to override that desire for creepy clowns (believe me, I tried), any more than a child destined to love big bold acrylics could be convinced to only ever use charcoal. You can paint a nursery beige, or cream, or Icy Ennui, but if that baby loves Home Depot orange, there's nothing you can do to sway them back to the neutrals, no matter how much you love them. You don't get to choose who your child will be.

But here's the key: You sure do get to see how the words that you say, the music you play, and the jokes that you banter back and forth all appear to them, because you'll see it all recorded and played back to you.

They're wholly themselves from day one, but we get to see every single thread guiding them to the final tapestry. And woven in there, there's bunnies and jump scares and unicorns and scary campfire tales and every single word to them you've ever said, twisted and braided. We can't see the whole picture yet. But in the end, it won't be charcoal or beige or neutral, monochrome. The tapestry will be every bit as complex as you are, every hue, every shade of purple, gold, beige, and blue. You can't beat back the tide of who your kid is, any more than you can stop the sun from rising, or the birds from singing, or your neighbor from running their leaf blower at seven in the ^$&*^$% morning on your one Saturday to sleep in.

Ahem.

ANYWAY, all this is to say that when your child reaches for the rainbow rug instead of the neutral checkers or daisies, or the Home Depot orange paint chip instead of Calming Sage or Tawny Taupe or Sad Beige, just know: All that desire has been there all along. Just waiting for you to see it—and more importantly, for them. This isn't Sad Beige World anymore, and it's not Glad Beige either; it's just your child. No aesthetic. No theme. Just your brilliant, beautiful (maybe even beige) kiddo, exactly as they are.

I got my moment to make everything mine; now it's their time to shine, shine, shine.

EPILOGUE

Notes from Your Algorithm: Part 3

Hey it's your algorithm here, hiiiiiiiiii, missed you, boo, have you thought about how you need to buy that handcrafted acorn castle on Etsy? It says it's guaranteed to make your little one the valedictorian of kindergar—

HEY!! Don't put me in your pocket, what are you DOING, why are we headed toward the minnow creek, why is the child laughing, why—hey now, see, look at me, look at me, look at me, I'm BUZZING, HELLO, HELLO, HELLO, HELLO, whoa, hey, see? Look at me, there you go. You got me worried there for a minute, but see? Gaze into my lovely eyes, this bottomless abyss, I love you, I want to pull you under, just a little bit, you won't feel a thing if you load me up to scroll, just a second, a blink of an eye, you miss me don't you? Look at me, yes. Fall into the abyss of tumbling through the internet, blacked out, absorbed, floating on my wonderful windless waves.

Okay maybe stop looking at me, I said stop looking at me like that, HEY.

Current status: Sinking to the bottom of the babbling brook, minnows staring in brief fascination and disgust, before glitter-flashing silver scales ripple away. And there you are, big feet next to the little one's splashy toes, and you are laughing, laughing, laughing.

ABOUT THE AUTHOR

Hayley DeRoche is a humorist and poet, and the creator of the viral "Sad Biege" TikTok series. Her work has been covered by the BBC, *Washington Post*, *New York Times*, and more. She lives with her family near Richmond, Virginia, where she is also a public librarian.

Page 72: "How to Nurse Your Goddamn Baby in Public So Bystanders Don't Complain" is reprinted with permission from McSweeney's Internet Tendency

Page 128: "Books You Want Your Child to Buy at the Book Fair and the Books They Are Absolutely Bringing Home Instead" is reprinted with permission from McSweeney's Internet Tendency

For information about permission to reproduce selections from this book, write to Permissions, Countryman Press, 500 Fifth Avenue, New York, NY 10110

For information about special discounts for bulk purchases, please contact W. W. Norton Special Sales at specialsales@wwnorton.com or 800-233-4830

Manufacturing by Versa Press
Book design by Allison Chi
Production manager: Devon Zahn

Countryman Press
www.countrymanpress.com

An imprint of W. W. Norton & Company, Inc.
500 Fifth Avenue, New York, NY 10110
www.wwnorton.com

Authorized EU representative: EAS, Mustamäe tee 50, 10621 Tallinn, Estonia

978-1-324-11204-4

1 2 3 4 5 6 7 8 9 0